PIANO • VOCAL • GUITAR

Sarah McLachlan
afterglow

P9-DFL-988

ISBN 0-634-07312-5

HAL•LEONARD® CORPORATION

7777 W. BLUEMOUND RD. P.O. BOX 13819 MILWAUKEE, WI 53213

For all works contained herein:
Unauthorized copying, arranging, adapting, recording or public performance is an infringement of copyright.
Infringers are liable under the law.

Visit Hal Leonard Online at
www.halleonard.com

FALLEN

Words and Music by
SARAH McLACHLAN

Moderately slow

Heav-en, bend to take my hand and lead me through the fire. Be the
Heav-en, bend to take my hand, I've no-where left to turn. I'm

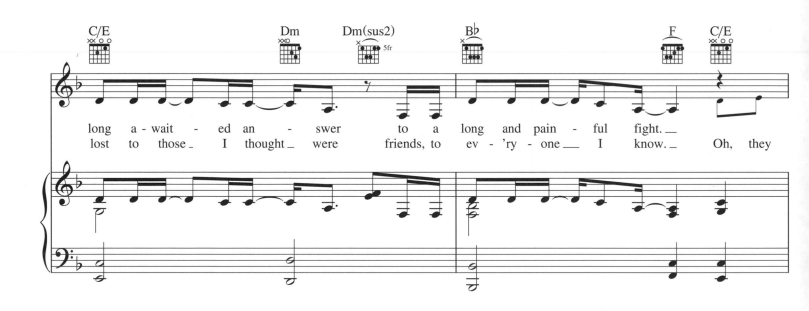

long a-wait-ed an-swer to a long and pain-ful fight.
lost to those I thought were friends, to ev-'ry-one I know. Oh, they

Truth be told, I've tried my best, but some-where a-long the way I
turn their heads, em-bar-rassed, pre-tend that they don't see, but it's

Copyright © 2003 Sony/ATV Songs LLC and Tyde Music
All Rights Administered by Sony/ATV Music Publishing, 8 Music Square West, Nashville, TN 37203
International Copyright Secured   All Rights Reserved

To Coda ⊕

so don't _ come _ 'round here and tell me I _ told _ you so. _

We

all be - gin _ with good _ in - tent. Love was raw _ and young. _ We be -

lieved that we _ could change _ our - selves, _ the past can be un - done. _ But we

WORLD ON FIRE

Words and Music by SARAH McLACHLAN
and PIERRE MARCHAND

Hearts __ are worn __ in these __ dark a - ges.
I watch the heav - ens for my fi - nal call - ing.

You're not __ a - lone __ in this
Some - thing I can do __ to

Copyright © 2003 Sony/ATV Songs LLC, Tyde Music and Studio Nomade Music
All Rights on behalf of Sony/ATV Songs LLC and Tyde Music Administered by Sony/ATV Music Publishing, 8 Music Square West, Nashville, TN 37203
International Copyright Secured   All Rights Reserved

less we be-come. The for-tune of one __ man means less for some.

The

STUPID

Words and Music by
SARAH McLACHLAN

Copyright © 2003 Sony/ATV Songs LLC and Tyde Music
All Rights Administered by Sony/ATV Music Publishing, 8 Music Square West, Nashville, TN 37203
International Copyright Secured   All Rights Reserved

DRIFTING

Words and Music by
SARAH McLACHLAN

You've been gone so long that all that you know ___ has been

shuf - fled a - side ___ as you bask in the glow of the

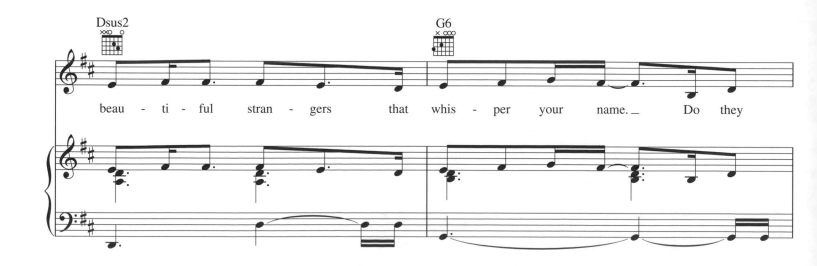

beau - ti - ful stran - gers that whis - per your name. ___ Do they

Copyright © 2003 Sony/ATV Songs LLC and Tyde Music
All Rights Administered by Sony/ATV Music Publishing, 8 Music Square West, Nashville, TN 37203
International Copyright Secured All Rights Reserved

TRAINWRECK

Words and Music by
SARAH McLACHLAN

*The vocal part is written an octave higher than it sounds.

Lyrics:
Would your love, ___ in all ___ its fin - 'ry, tear at the dark - ness all ___
Would your eyes, ___ like mid - night fire - flies, light up the trench - es where ___
From your mouth, ___ it's all ___ that I ___ wish; the mer - cy of your ___ lips, just ___

Copyright © 2003 Sony/ATV Songs LLC and Tyde Music
All Rights Administered by Sony/ATV Music Publishing, 8 Music Square West, Nashville, TN 37203
International Copyright Secured   All Rights Reserved

PUSH

Words and Music by
SARAH McLACHLAN

Moderately slow

Ev-'ry time I look at you, the world just melts a - way.
I get mad so eas - y, but you give me room to breathe, no
There are times I can't de - cide, when I can't tell up from down. You

All my trou - bles, all my fears dis - solve in your af - fec - tions. You've
mat - ter what I say or do, 'cause you're too good to fight a - bout it.
make me feel less cra - zy, when oth - er - wise I'd drown. But you

seen me at my weak - est, but you take me as I am, and
E - ven when I have to push, just to see how far you'll go, you
pick me up and brush me off and tell me I'm o - kay.

Copyright © 2003 Sony/ATV Songs LLC and Tyde Music
All Rights Administered by Sony/ATV Music Publishing, 8 Music Square West, Nashville, TN 37203
International Copyright Secured All Rights Reserved

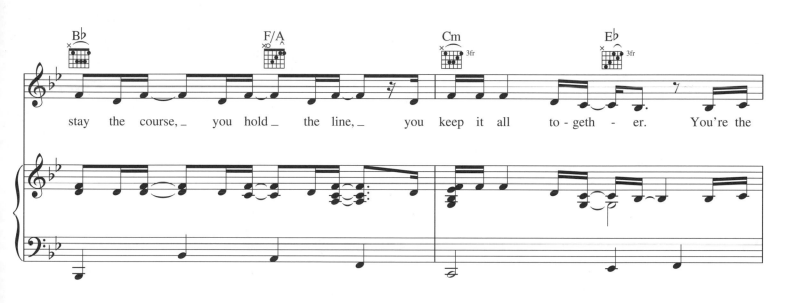

34

stay the course, _ you hold _ the line, _ you keep it all to - geth - er. You're the

one true thing I know I can _ be - lieve. _

Repeat and Fade

Optional Ending

ANSWER

Words and Music by
SARAH McLACHLAN

Lyrics:
I will be the an- swer at the end of ___ the line. I will be there for __

Copyright © 2003 Sony/ATV Songs LLC and Tyde Music
All Rights Administered by Sony/ATV Music Publishing, 8 Music Square West, Nashville, TN 37203
International Copyright Secured   All Rights Reserved

TIME

Words and Music by
SARAH McLACHLAN

*Female vocal written one octave higher than sung

Copyright © 2003 Sony/ATV Songs LLC and Tyde Music
All Rights Administered by Sony/ATV Music Publishing, 8 Music Square West, Nashville, TN 37203
International Copyright Secured   All Rights Reserved

Guitar solo ad lib.

loco

Solo ends

Time here _____ all but means noth - ing, just _____

shad - ows that move _____ 'cross the wall. _____

PERFECT GIRL

Words and Music by SARAH McLACHLAN
and PIERRE MARCHAND

Am I faith - ful, am ____ I strong, ____ am I good e - nough
own my in - se - cur - i - ties; ____ I try to own my ____
ri - ot in ____ my heart ____ de - cides ____ to keep me o - pen ____

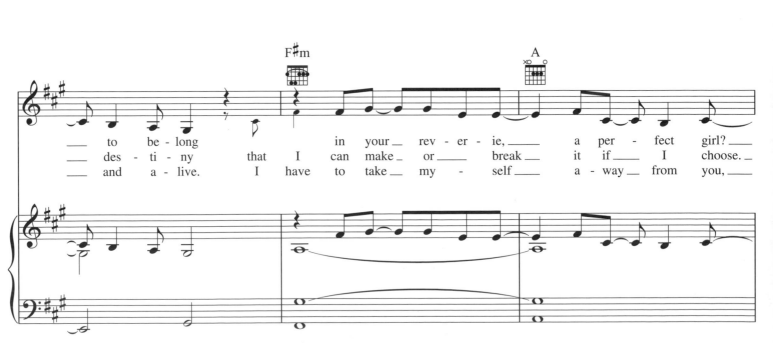

____ to be - long in your ____ rev - er - ie, ____ a per - fect girl? ____
____ des - ti - ny that I can make ____ or ____ break ____ it if ____ I choose. ____
____ and a - live. I have to take ____ my - self ____ a - way ____ from you, ____

Copyright © 2003 Sony/ATV Songs LLC, Tyde Music and Studio Nomade Music
All Rights on behalf of Sony/ATV Songs LLC and Tyde Music Administered by Sony/ATV Music Publishing, 8 Music Square West, Nashville, TN 37203
International Copyright Secured   All Rights Reserved

DIRTY LITTLE SECRET

Words and Music by
SARAH McLACHLAN

Copyright © 2003 Sony/ATV Songs LLC and Tyde Music
All Rights Administered by Sony/ATV Music Publishing, 8 Music Square West, Nashville, TN 37203
International Copyright Secured All Rights Reserved